Where is your Faith?

Father, we say thank You for the times that You have not given up on us and when we doubted and didn't want to trust You for whatever reason. Lord, You didn't give up on us, You still brought Your spoken words to pass, in spite of our unbelief and our ill spoken words concerning our present state. You still remained God. You didn't give up or remove from Your position as God and for that we say thank you, thank you and thank you!

May You find it in Your heart to forgive us for our thoughts and deeds, and as we read this book may we experience an increase in our faith to the point of no longer looking back and discussing what others say and feel. May we hold on to who You are, what is spoken and written. I thank You today for the ever-increasing faith and trust in You, in Jesus Name, Amen.

1

Table of Content

Hebrews 11:1 **"NOW faith is the Assurance of things hoped for and the evidence of things not seen."**

Greek meaning:

persuasion example moral conviction.

English meaning:

Strong belief in the doctrine of a religion based on spiritual conviction rather than proof.

Introduction

Faith is the action to the spoken word. Faith comes by hearing (so where is your word). The Lord told Abraham to go from among them to a place that I will show you. He believed God. His faith was activated. He moved on the word.

Hence there was a manifestation of the spoken word. He received the word by faith and acted. He didn't doubt, fear, or show unbelief. We must understand our actions and words are manifestation of the Spirit we sometimes carry.

In other words what we do and what we say tells what spirit is in operation in our lives. The lack of belief and faith is contrary to the Christian faith. We must be at a place in God where we can stand on His word, believing all that He said whether we can comprehend it or not. At times, we may not understand how the Lord may bring a thing to pass, but know that this is not our job to understand how, where, when or who He will use.

Our position should be that of faith, if God said it, I receive it and that settles it.

It is in our faith and trust in the Most High God that things will happen and surely come to pass.

It is my prayer for you dear reader, that after reading this book your faith will arise and be sustained in Jesus Mighty Name.

We can have a word and a spirit come in and demolish the word.

The Spirit of Fear

Definition of fear;

Fear is an emotion induced by perceived danger or threat, which causes physiological changes and ultimately behavioral changes, such as fleeing, hiding, or freezing from perceived traumatic events.

This spirit brings fear of the unknown, fear of the future and fear of the present. Fear of what others feel and think about you. Fear of not succeeding in a thing, fear of changes, (fear of stepping out, so you remain in a box).

Here are some scriptures to meditate upon.

Matthew 10:28 **"And do not be afraid of those who kill the body but cannot kill the soul; but rather be afraid of Him who can destroy both soul and body in hell (Gehenna)."**

Isaiah 54:4 **"Fear not, for you shall not be ashamed; neither be confounded and depressed, for you shall not be put to shame. For you shall forget the shame of your youth, and you shall not [seriously] remember the reproach of your widowhood anymore."**

Isaiah 41:10 **"Fear not [there is nothing to fear], for I am with you; do not look around you in terror and be dismayed, for I am your God. I will strengthen and harden you to difficulties, yes, I will help you; yes, I will hold you up and retain you with My [victorious] right hand of rightness and justice. [Acts 18:10.]"**

Psalm 56:3 **"What time I am afraid, I will have confidence in and put my trust and reliance in You."**

Psalm 56:4 **"By [the help of] God I will praise His word; on God I lean, rely, and confidently put my trust; I will not fear. What can man, who is flesh, do to me?"**

Deuteronomy 31:6 **"Be strong, courageous, and firm; fear not nor be in terror before them, for it is the Lord your God Who goes with you; He will not fail you or forsake you."**

Psalm 118:6 **"The Lord is on my side; I will not fear. What can man do to me? [Heb. 13:6.]"**

Psalm 27:1 **"THE Lord is my Light and my Salvation—whom shall I fear or dread? The Lord is the Refuge and Stronghold of my life—of whom shall I be afraid?"**

Psalm 94:19 **"In the multitude of my [anxious] thoughts within me, Your comforts cheer and delight my soul!"**

Isaiah 43:1 "**BUT NOW [in spite of past judgments for Israel's sins], thus says the Lord, He Who created you, O Jacob, and He Who formed you, O Israel: Fear not, for I have redeemed you [ransomed you by paying a price instead of leaving you captives]; I have called you by your name; you are Mine.**"

Joshua 1:9 "**Have not I commanded you? Be strong, vigorous, and very courageous. Be not afraid, neither be dismayed, for the Lord your God is with you wherever you go.**"

Prophet's Prayer of Deliverance from the Spirit of Fear

Father in the name of Jesus Christ, we come before You Lord, asking You to remove and cancel the spirit of fear and anxiety from off the life of this person in the Name of Jesus Christ.

Whatever plans that the enemy has to hinder this person from moving forward, I ask that You free them and not allow this spirit to return in the Name of Jesus. For Your word declares that You have not given us the spirit of fear. Fear is not of You; we don't want it in our lives. We want to be bold soldiers working for Your kingdom.

God may You help us to see ourselves the way You see us in Jesus Mighty and Precious Name, we pray, Amen.

The Spirit of Unbelief

Definition of unbelief;

lack of religious belief, an absence of faith.

It is my belief that because one hasn't seen things done a particular way before, they shut it down in their minds. They say "I do not believe it, it cannot be."

Prophet's Prayer of Deliverance from the Spirit of Unbelief

Most Gracious and Eternal Father, we bless and praise Your Name today. For You alone are God and besides You, there is no other. Father, I ask today and every day of my life that You would address the spirit of unbelief. Deliver me and move it far away. Help me to hold on to Your word, and to accept and believe without hesitation. Teach me how to stand on Your word that is declared in the book of Jude 1:22, "And refute [so as to] convict some who dispute with you, and on some have mercy who waver and doubt." It is my desire not to be taken away by the wind. I ask Lord that You would keep me from wavering and doubt. That I may become a firm, strong and steady believer. In Jesus Mighty and Precious Name I pray, Amen.

The Spirit of Doubt

Definition of doubt;

A feeling of uncertainty or lack of conviction.

If you are not knowledgeable in this area, this information can bring a different revelation from what you receive versus what one who tends to doubt the information or the demonstration of the Spirit of God.

John 20:24-31

John 20:24 **"But Thomas, one of the Twelve, called the Twin, was not with them when Jesus came."**

John 20:25 **"So the other disciples kept telling him, We have seen the Lord! But he said to them, Unless I see in His hands the marks made by the nails and put my finger into the nail prints, and put my hand into His side, I will never believe [it]."**

John 20:26 **"Eight days later His disciples were again in the house, and Thomas was with them. Jesus came, though they were behind closed doors, and stood among them and said, Peace to you!"**

John 20:27 **"Then He said to Thomas, Reach out your finger here, and see My hands; and put out your hand and place [it] in My side. Do not be faithless and incredulous, but [stop your unbelief and] believe!"**

John 20:28 **"Thomas answered Him, My Lord and my God!"**

John 20:29 **"Jesus said to him, Because you have seen Me, Thomas, do you now believe (trust, have faith)? Blessed and happy and to be envied are those who have never seen Me and yet have believed and adhered to and trusted and relied on Me."**

John 20:30 **"There are also many other signs and miracles which Jesus performed in the presence of the disciples which are not written in this book."**

John 20:31 **"But these are written (recorded) in order that you may believe that Jesus is the Christ (the Anointed One), the Son of God, and that through believing and cleaving to and trusting and relying upon Him you may have life through (in) His name [through Who He is]. [Ps. 2:7, 12.]"**

When we look at these scriptures we see where Thomas doubted because he refused to believe that the resurrected Jesus had been seen by other Apostles until he could actually see and feel the wounds that He (Jesus) had received on the cross.

Spiritual nugget

Yesterday's faith will not do. Last month's faith will not do. But NOW faith, In this moment and time.

Let's look at the story of Zachariah in the Bible in Luke 1:18-20.

Luke 1:18 **"And Zachariah said to the angel, By what shall I know and be sure of this? For I am an old man, and my wife is well advanced in years."**

Luke 1:19 **"And the angel replied to him, I am Gabriel. I stand in the [very] presence of God, and I have been sent to talk to you and to bring you this good news. [Dan. 8:16; 9:21.]"**

Luke 1:20 **"Now behold, you will be and will continue to be silent and not able to speak till the day when these things take place, because you have not believed what I told you; but my words are of a kind which will be fulfilled in the appointed and proper time."**

As we look deeper into this, we see where upon the visit of the angel when he told Zachariah of the plan God had concerning, he and his wife.

Zachariah's first response was the age of both he and his wife. It tells me in not so many words that he thought they were just too old to get pregnant. In other words, he thought it impossible, he doubted.

Hence, an order to keep his mouth shut, from speaking doubt was ordered by God until the time for the word to come forth and manifest what was spoken by God concerning him and his wife.

It is my belief that we as believers should all try to keep the faith on that which God has spoken.

Here are a few scriptures to meditate upon concerning doubt.

Proverbs 3:5-8.

Proverbs 3:5 **"Lean on, trust in, and be confident in the Lord with all your heart and mind and do not rely on your own insight or understanding."**

Proverbs 3:6 **"In all your ways know, recognize, and acknowledge Him, and He will direct and make straight and plain your paths."**

Proverbs 3:7 **"Be not wise in your own eyes; reverently fear and worship the Lord and turn [entirely] away from evil. [Prov. 8:13.]"**

Proverbs 3:8 **"It shall be health to your nerves and sinews, and marrow and moistening to your bones."**

James 1:6 **"Only it must be in faith that he asks with no wavering (no hesitating, no doubting). For the one who wavers (hesitates, doubts) is like the billowing surge out at sea that is blown hither and thither and tossed by the wind."**

Prophet's Prayer of Deliverance from the Spirit of Doubt

You alone Oh God, are the one true God. There is none like You Father, I place my life, and my innermost being in Your care. You are the King of kings and the Lord of lords, none can comparison to You Oh righteous Lord and Savior. I humbly bow down before You in total submission unto to You Oh God asking You Lord to X-ray me. Today, and remove this spirit of doubt that seeks to stop me from being who You have called me to be. Lord, I want to believe Your words and actions, and so I ask that by Your power, might and spirit remove everything in my life that isn't a part of Your plan for my life.

Whatsoever things that are planted by the enemy to bring about doubt in You Lord, and who You are, may You dismantle it. Master of all the universe, bring complete peace and assurance into my life in Jesus Name, Amen.

Bondage in the Mind

Definition of bondage:

The state of being a slave.

It is my personal belief, that when you're talking to people who believe in a limited god, you are sowing seeds into your hearing of a god who is confound to boundaries.

 I believe this decreases your imagination of how big God really is, His power and authority. You see, your mind will not be extended if you continue on this path.

It's like putting God in a definite area, to limit Him as to what, how, when or if He can show up.

Let's take off the limits, all conditions and stop rationalizing in our mind about this Great and Mighty God.

Allow Him in His utmost Glory to be God.

Here are some scriptures to meditate upon.

Luke 4:18 **"The Spirit of the Lord [is] upon Me, because He has anointed Me [the Anointed One, the Messiah] to preach the good news (the Gospel) to the poor; He has sent Me to announce release to the captives and recovery of sight to the blind, to send forth as delivered those who are oppressed [who are downtrodden, bruised, crushed, and broken down by calamity],"**

Psalm 22:4 **"Our fathers trusted in You; they trusted (leaned on, relied on You, and were confident) and You delivered them."**

Psalm 32:7 **"You are a hiding place for me; You, Lord, preserve me from trouble, You surround me with songs and shouts of deliverance. Selah [pause, and calmly think of that]!"**

Proverbs 28:26 **"He who leans on, trusts in, and is confident of his own mind and heart is a [self-confident] fool, but he who walks in skillful and godly Wisdom shall be delivered. [James 1:5.]"**

Isaiah 49:24 **"Shall the prey be taken from the mighty, or the lawful captives of the just be delivered?"**

Isaiah 49:25 **"For thus says the Lord: Even the captives of the mighty will be taken away, and the prey of the terrible will be delivered; for I will contend with him who contends with you, and I will give safety to your children and ease them."**

Prophet's Prayer of Deliverance from the Spirit of Bondage

Most merciful Father, loving and caring in all of Your ways. We want to thank You for being Lord over our lives and helping us in areas we don't even know that we need help at times.

You God are the All-Knowing God. We bring all of our concerns before You that You may bring a conclusion that only You can.

Spirit of the living God, I bring my mind before You this day, every area of my mind. Things that are premature in thought and mature, asking You to cultivate my thinking that my mind and thoughts will stay upon You and allow You to bring me into maturity as to whom You have called me to.

Asking You Lord for a renewed mind daily. A productive mind in the spirit, one that is led by Your sweet Holy Spirit. Teach me Lord, how to seek You in all things, then to follow Your way. In Jesus Mighty and Precious Name, I pray, Amen.

- A word that is to be planted, must be allowed to take root and grow.
- It must be planted in good soil. It needs sunlight, rain, and to be nourished, in order to grow.
- The word (spoken word) must be in the light, no darkness. No dark opinions, no dark ideas or dark conclusions.
- The rain (the word must be blessed).
- Nourished (day after day you must remind God of His word.
- That the word may come forth in its set timing and season.
- A word doesn't just come from a Prophet or pastor. A son, daughter, neighbor or even a total stranger can give you a word from the Lord.
- But when you say i don't receive that or I don't believe that, this spirit automatically goes into operation. (spirit of fear, doubt, unbelief, bondage in the mind).

Spiritual nugget

You need a word from God in order to have faith. You cannot say am having faith for a house, if God didn't say, I will give you a house.

Where is your faith?

Do you have the now faith?

Unmovable, unshakeable Faith. The kind of faith that doesn't move or shake because of our current or past situations, but remains in tack. The kind of faith that will endure patience to the very end.

Faith for the Supernatural

Definition:

Is that which is not subject to the law of nature or more figuratively, that which is said to exist above and beyond nature.

Matthew 14:26-30

Matthew 14:26 **"When the disciples saw him walking on the sea, they were terrified, and said, it is a ghost! And they cried out in fear."**

Matthew 14:27 **"But immediately He spoke to them and saying, "take courage, it is I! Do not be afraid!"**

Matthew 14:28 **"Peter replied to him, "Lord if it is you, command me to come to you on the water."**

Matthew 14:29 **"He said, "come!" so Peter got out of the boat, and walked on the water and came toward Jesus."**

Matthew 14:30 **"But when he saw the wind, he was frightened, and he began to sink, and he cried out, "Lord save me!"**

In the scriptures we understand that Peter and those that saw Jesus walking on the water, thought it was a ghost. They were so afraid to acknowledge it was Jesus.

Being filled with faith, Peter asked Jesus, command me to come. Jesus did, and Peter got out of the boat and began walking on water.

It is my belief that Peter went from the supernatural to the natural in those moments and began to sink. I believe once he took his eyes off of Jesus, fear began to access in his mind.

I believe the spirit of fear came in at that point. Then he feared and began to sink.

In today society we see this oh too many times, where God can begin using people in such a powerful way but for one reason or another, the movements in the realm of the spirit decreases, or comes to a full stop.

Sometimes, it can be because of the opinion of mankind concerning that individual and the way God chooses to use them. It can have a tremendous impact on an individual's life. (If they choose to continually push forward or pull back)

Faith in the Supernatural to be Healed

Luke 8:43-48

Luke 8:43 **"Now a woman was there who had been suffering from a hemorrhage for twelve years but could not be healed by anyone."**

Luke 8:44 **"She came up behind Jesus and touched the edge of his cloak, and at once the bleeding stopped."**

Luke 8:45 **"Then Jesus asked, "Who was it who touched me?" When they all denied it, Peter said, "Master, the crowds are surrounding you and pressing against you!"**

Luke 8:46 **"But Jesus said, "Someone touched me, for I know that power has gone out from me."**

Luke 8:47 **"When the woman saw that she could not escape notice, she came trembling and fell down before him. In the presence of all the people, she explained why she had touched him and how she had been immediately healed."**

Luke 8:48 **"Then he said to her, "Daughter, your faith has made you well. Go in peace."**

When we look at scripture, here we find out that this woman that was once sick was not concerned about the protocol that was probably already in place. She was not concerned about what people would say about her or her condition, her faith was in Jesus to heal her.

She wasn't bothered by who the person was, if you think they were qualify or what church he was from. If he was Baptist or catholic. She knew that God was using Him and she needed her healing.

Sometimes persons can come up to the altar, but still have no faith, doubting in their minds, if it's possible to be heal.

There is a measure of faith that is needed in order for the supernatural to take place.

We must believe that God can, He is the healer (Jehovah Rapha) working through persons.

Faith to Lead

Moses went to Egypt to lead the Israelites out. He got a word from the Lord, this equipped him in the spirit. He just needed to follow orders.

Faith is actioning on what God said.

There are times you will be called upon to lead others. They maybe disobedient to your orders, but this doesn't mean that you are a failed leader or not one that God has called as a leader.

The actions of others don't dictate who you are and if you are called. I believe the Israelites were supposed to journey for eleven days, but the journey actually took them fourth years.

This always puzzled me to what could have been the reasons for their delay. Did it have to do with the leader or was it really themselves?

Sometimes we can be our own hindrance because of our mind set, it stops us from moving forward.

When we experience a level of doubt within ourselves and even fear of what to expect in the days and months ahead, this can stagnant our growth and progress.

A true leader must lead and those that are called to follow, must follow with integrity.

Faith to Stand

Have or Maintain an Upright Position

Three Hebrew boys. Daniel 3:8-30.

Daniel 3:8 **"Therefore at that time certain men of Chaldean descent came near and brought [malicious] accusations against the Jews."**

Daniel 3:9 **"They said to King Nebuchadnezzar, O king, live forever!"**

Daniel 3:10 **"You, O king, have made a decree that every man who hears the sound of the horn, pipe, lyre, trigon, harp, dulcimer or bagpipe, and every kind of music shall fall down and worship the golden image,"**

Daniel 3:11 **"And that whoever does not fall down and worship shall be cast into the midst of a burning fiery furnace."**

Daniel 3:12 **"There are certain Jews whom you have appointed and set over the affairs of the province of Babylon— Shadrach, Meshach, and Abednego. These men, O king, pay no attention to you; they do not serve your gods or worship the golden image which you have set up."**

Daniel 3:13 **"Then Nebuchadnezzar in rage and fury commanded to bring Shadrach, Meshach, and Abednego; and these men were brought before the king."**

Daniel 3:14 **"[Then] Nebuchadnezzar said to them, Is it true, O Shadrach, Meshach, and Abednego, that you do not serve my gods or worship the golden image which I have set up?"**

Daniel 3:15 **"Now if you are ready when you hear the sound of the horn, pipe, lyre, trigon, harp, dulcimer or bagpipe, and every kind of music to fall down and worship the image which I have made, very good. But if you do not worship, you shall be cast at once into the midst of a burning fiery furnace, and who is that god who can deliver you out of my hands?"**

Daniel 3:16 **"Shadrach, Meshach, and Abednego answered the king, O Nebuchadnezzar, it is not necessary for us to answer you on this point."**

Daniel 3:17 **"If our God Whom we serve is able to deliver us from the burning fiery furnace, He will deliver us out of your hand, O king."**

Daniel 3:18 **"But if not, let it be known to you, O king, that we will not serve your gods or worship the golden image which you have set up! [Job 13:15; Acts 4:19, 20.]"**

Daniel 3:19 **"Then Nebuchadnezzar was full of fury and his facial expression was changed [to antagonism] against Shadrach, Meshach, and Abednego. Therefore he commanded that the furnace should be heated seven times hotter than it was usually heated."**

Daniel 3:20 **"And he commanded the strongest men in his army to bind Shadrach, Meshach, and Abednego and to cast them into the burning fiery furnace."**

Daniel 3:21 **"Then these [three] men were bound in their cloaks, their tunics or undergarments, their turbans, and their other clothing, and they were cast into the midst of the burning fiery furnace."**

Daniel 3:22 **"Therefore because the king's commandment was urgent and the furnace exceedingly hot, the flame and sparks from the fire killed those men who handled Shadrach, Meshach, and Abednego."**

Daniel 3:23 **"And these three men, Shadrach, Meshach, and Abednego, fell down bound into the burning fiery furnace."**

Daniel 3:24 "**Then Nebuchadnezzar the king [saw and] was astounded, and he jumped up and said to his counselors, Did we not cast three men bound into the midst of the fire? They answered, True, O king.**"

Daniel 3:25 "**He answered, Behold, I see four men loose, walking in the midst of the fire, and they are not hurt! And the form of the fourth is like a son of the gods! [Phil. 2:5-8.]**"

Daniel 3:26 "**Then Nebuchadnezzar came near to the mouth of the burning fiery furnace and said, Shadrach, Meshach, and Abednego, you servants of the Most High God, come out and come here. Then Shadrach, Meshach, and Abednego came out from the midst of the fire.**"

Daniel 3:27 "**And the satraps, the deputies, the governors, and the king's counselors gathered around together and saw these men—that the fire had no power upon their bodies, nor was the hair of their head singed; neither were their garments scorched or changed in color or condition, nor had even the smell of smoke clung to them.**"

Daniel 3:28 **"Then Nebuchadnezzar said, Blessed be the God of Shadrach, Meshach, and Abednego, Who has sent His angel and delivered His servants who believed in, trusted in, and relied on Him! And they set aside the king's command and yielded their bodies rather than serve or worship any god except their own God."**

Daniel 3:29 **"Therefore I make a decree that any people, nation, and language that speaks anything amiss against the God of Shadrach, Meshach, and Abednego shall be cut in pieces and their houses be made a dunghill, for there is no other God who can deliver in this way!"**

Daniel 3:30 **"Then the king promoted Shadrach, Meshach, and Abednego in the province of Babylon."**

Spiritual nugget

Without faith it is impossible to please God. This is why God referred to Abraham as his friend, because of Abraham's faith.

Faith to Produce

Cause to Happen or Exist

Sarah; Hebrew 11:11

"By faith even Sarah herself received the ability to conceive (a child), even when she was long past the normal age for it, because she considered Him who had given her the promise to be reliable and true (to his word)."

Faith to Fight

Struggle to Overcome, Eliminate, or Prevent

Gideon

Judges 7:1 **"THEN JERUBBAAL, that is, Gideon, and all the people who were with him rose early and encamped beside the spring of Harod; and the camp of Midian was north of them by the hill of Moreh in the valley."**

Judges 7:2 **"The Lord said to Gideon, The people who are with you are too many for Me to give the Midianites into their hands, lest Israel boast about themselves against Me, saying, My own hand has delivered me."**

Judges 7:3 **"So now proclaim in the ears of the men, saying, Whoever is fearful and trembling, let him turn back and depart from Mount Gilead. And 22,000 of the men returned, but 10,000 remained."**

Judges 7:4 **"And the Lord said to Gideon, The men are still too many; bring them down to the water, and I will test them for you there. And he of whom I say to you, This man shall go with you, shall go with you; and he of whom I say to you, This man shall not go with you, shall not go."**

Judges 7:5 **"So he brought the men down to the water, and the Lord said to Gideon, Everyone who laps up the water with his tongue as a dog laps it, you shall set by himself, likewise everyone who bows down on his knees to drink."**

Judges 7:6 **"And the number of those who lapped, putting their hand to their mouth, was 300 men, but all the rest of the people bowed down upon their knees to drink water."**

Judges 7:7 **"And the Lord said to Gideon, With the 300 men who lapped I will deliver you, and give the Midianites into your hand. Let all the others return every man to his home."**

Judges 7:8 **"So the people took provisions and their trumpets in their hands, and he sent all the rest of Israel every man to his home and retained those 300 men. And the host of Midian was below him in the valley."**

Judges 7:9 **"That same night the Lord said to Gideon, Arise, go down against their camp, for I have given it into your hand."**

Judges 7:10 **"But if you fear to go down, go with Purah your servant down to the camp"**

Judges 7:11 **"And you shall hear what they say, and afterward your hands shall be strengthened to go down against the camp. Then he went down with Purah his servant to the outposts of the camp of the armed men."**

Judges 7:12 **"And the Midianites and the Amalekites and all the sons of the east lay along the valley like locusts for multitude; and their camels were without number, as the sand on the seashore for multitude."**

Judges 7:13 "When Gideon arrived, behold, a man was telling a dream to his comrade. And he said, Behold, I dreamed a dream, and behold, a cake of barley bread tumbled into the camp of Midian and came to the tent and struck it so that it fell, and turned it upside down so that the tent lay flat."

Judges 7:14 "And his comrade replied, This is nothing else but the sword of Gideon son of Joash, a man of Israel. Into his hand God has given Midian and all the host."

Judges 7:15 "When Gideon heard the telling of the dream and its interpretation, he worshiped and returned to the camp of Israel and said, Arise, for the Lord has given into your hand the host of Midian."

Judges 7:16 "And he divided the 300 men into three companies, and he put into the hands of all of them trumpets and empty pitchers, with torches inside the pitchers."

Judges 7:17 "And he said to them, Look at me, then do likewise. When I come to the edge of their camp, do as I do."

Judges 7:18 **"When I blow the trumpet, I and all who are with me, then you blow the trumpets also on every side of all the camp and shout, For the Lord and for Gideon!"**

Judges 7:19 **"So Gideon and the 100 men who were with him came to the outskirts of the camp at the beginning of the middle watch, when the guards had just been changed, and they blew the trumpets and smashed the pitchers that were in their hands."**

Judges 7:20 **"And the three companies blew the trumpets and shattered the pitchers, holding the torches in their left hands, and in their right hands the trumpets to blow [leaving no chance to use swords], and they cried, The sword for the Lord and Gideon!"**

Judges 7:21 **"They stood every man in his place round about the camp, and all the [Midianite] army ran–they cried out and fled."**

Judges 7:22 **"When [Gideon's men] blew the 300 trumpets, the Lord set every [Midianite's] sword against his comrade and against all the army, and the army fled as far as Beth-shittah toward Zererah, as far as the border of Abel-meholah by Tabbath."**

Judges 7:23 **"And the men of Israel were called together out of Naphtali and Asher and all Manasseh, and they pursued Midian."**

Judges 7:24 **"And Gideon sent messengers throughout all the hill country of Ephraim, saying, Come down against the Midianites and take all the intervening fords as far as Beth-barah and also the Jordan. So all the men of Ephraim were gathered together and took all the fords as far as Beth-barah and also the Jordan."**

When we read in scripture, we see that the Lord sent the angel to Gideon. Gideon asked how can I save Israel I am nothing, The Lord told him, I will give you the victory.

But you have too much soldiers, you may think you won the fight by yourself. The Lord said to tell everyone that is afraid to go home. (there must be a separation because fear is not of God) Twenty-two thousand went home.

 Then take the remains to the stream and tell them to drink. Now keep with you, only those who drink and are watchful (alert for the enemy) and that is all we are taking to war. Those that are strategic in their watchfulness of the enemy and doesn't carry a spirit of fear.

This is who God qualified (them) to be a part of the army. (even in the army of the Lord, we must be watchful and alert.) No matter what is going on to always have an eye for the enemy. Keeping ourselves positioned in prayer to know what God is saying concerning us. When and how to move concerning thing to come.

Also, understanding that not every fight will be fought the same way. The Lord sometimes uses different methods to get the same results.

Faith to Crossover to the Promise Land

a place or situation in which someone expects to find great happiness.

Joshua 1:1-2. God's commission to Joshua.

Joshua 1:1 **"Now it happened after the death of Moses the servant of the Lord, that the Lord spoke to Joshua the son of nun, servant (attendant), saying,"**

Joshua 1:2 **"Moses my servant is dead; now therefore arise (to take his place), cross over this Jordan, you and all this people, into the land which I am giving to them, to the sons of Israel."**

In the scriptures we learn that Joshua didn't seek council (from man), he receives the word by faith and acted upon it. He was charged to arise, come forth and to lead God people.

The Lord didn't question him about the amount of people that didn't like him or who in society disapprove of his appointment. He was asked to arise, and to take his position of authority.

There are something's that are predestined for you. But only by faith shall you receive. Faith to crossover to the promise land, like Joshua there was a said time for him to take action on the spoken word of God.

Faith in the Economy of Heaven

careful management of available resources

2 Kings 4:1-7. Multiplication of oil.

2 Kings 4:1 **"Now one of the wives of a man of the sons of the prophet's cried out of Elisha (for help), saying Your servant my husband is dead, and you know that your servant (reverently) feared the Lord; but the creditor is coming to take my two sons to be his slaves (in payment for a loan)."**

2 Kings 4:2 **"Elisha said to her, what shall I do for you? Tell me, "what do you have (of value) in the house?" She said, your maidservant has nothing in the house except a small jar of olive oil."**

2 Kings 4:3 **"Then he said, go, borrow containers from all your neighbors, empty containers- and not just a few."**

2 Kings 4:4 **"Then you shall go in and shut the door behind you and your sons, and pour out (the oil you have) into all these containers, and you shall set aside each one when it is full."**

2 Kings 4:5 **"So she left him and shut the door behind her and her sons, they were bringing her the containers as she poured (the oil)."**

2 Kings 4:6 **"When the containers were all full, she said to her son, Bring me another container. And he said to her, there is not a one left. Then the oil stopped(multiplying)."**

2 Kings 4:7 **"Then she came and told the man of God. He said, Go sell the oil and pay your debt, and you and your sons can live on the rest."**

I want to say to the body of Christ, there will be no multiplication, if a law is broken, if a principal isn't met. For example, tithes.

Every excuse why you don't pay tithes, (but still have your nails done, still have in wigs and still buying clothes that you really don't need or even have space in the closet for) and complaining that you are only making so much and cannot afford to pay tithes. Precious, you cannot afford to not pay tithes.

When you don't pay tithes, it leaves a door open for the enemy to gain entrance into your life. This also can attract the spirit of mammon (which brings on a love for money and the worship of money).

When the god of mammon is in operation in your life, there is no multiplications only subtractions. Which may take you to a season of dryness.

Ensure that you as a believer is doing what you are expected to be doing in order to be living a God fulfilling life. One that will be bringing honor and glory to the name of the Lord.

Jude 1:24-25

Jude 1:24 **"Now to Him Who is able to keep you without stumbling or slipping or falling, and to present [you] unblemished (blameless and faultless) before the presence of His glory in triumphant joy and exultation [with unspeakable, ecstatic delight]–"**

Jude 1:25 **"To the one only God, our Savior through Jesus Christ our Lord, be glory (splendor), majesty, might and dominion, and power and authority, before all time and now and forever (unto all the ages of eternity). Amen (so be it)."**

Made in the USA
Middletown, DE
27 November 2021

53531452R10033